THE MEDIA

MAGAZINES

Kim Walden

Wayland

The Media

Advertising
Book Publishing
Cinema
Magazines
The Pop Music Business
Newspapers
Radio
Television and Video

Series designer: David Armitage
Book designer: Ross George
Editor: Rhoda Nottridge

First published in 1988 by
Wayland (Publishers) Ltd
61 Western Road, Hove
East Sussex BN3 1JD, England

© Copyright 1988 Wayland (Publishers) Ltd

Phototypeset by Oliver Dawkins Ltd.,
Burgess Hill, West Sussex
Printed in Italy by G. Canale & C.S.p.A., Turin
Bound in France by AGM

British Library Cataloguing in Publication Data

Walden, Kim
  Magazines
  1. Magazines. For children
  I. Title   II. Series
  070.5'72

ISBN 1-85210-289-6

Contents

1. The development of magazines   4
2. How the industry works   11
3. Comics and teenage magazines   17
4. Music magazines and the alternative press   26
5. Women's magazines   31
6. Special-interest magazines and the future   38

    Glossary   45
    Booklist   46
    Further information   46
    Index   47

1 The development of magazines

Before comics and magazines existed, there were humorous picture books, ballad song sheets and calendars. The term 'magazine' was not used until the 1730s when Edward Cave published his *Gentleman's Magazine* in Britain. This new type of leisure journal was designed to entertain its readers with eyewitness accounts of crime and punishment and romantic stories.

It proved popular, and soon a female counterpart was published called *The Lady's Magazine,* which could be bound into volumes for book shelves. Public houses, barbers' shops and fashionable coffee houses in cities began to stock the popular newspapers and magazines which could be rented by the reader. The frequency of publication increased as magazine reading caught on. Journals published quarterly became monthlies which in turn became weekly magazines — such was the demand for reading matter.

Right *To keep readers' attention, stories were serialized in monthly issues. Poems, puzzles and even card tricks were included in early journals.*

Below *For a small sum a customer could relax with his favourite magazine and have a haircut.*

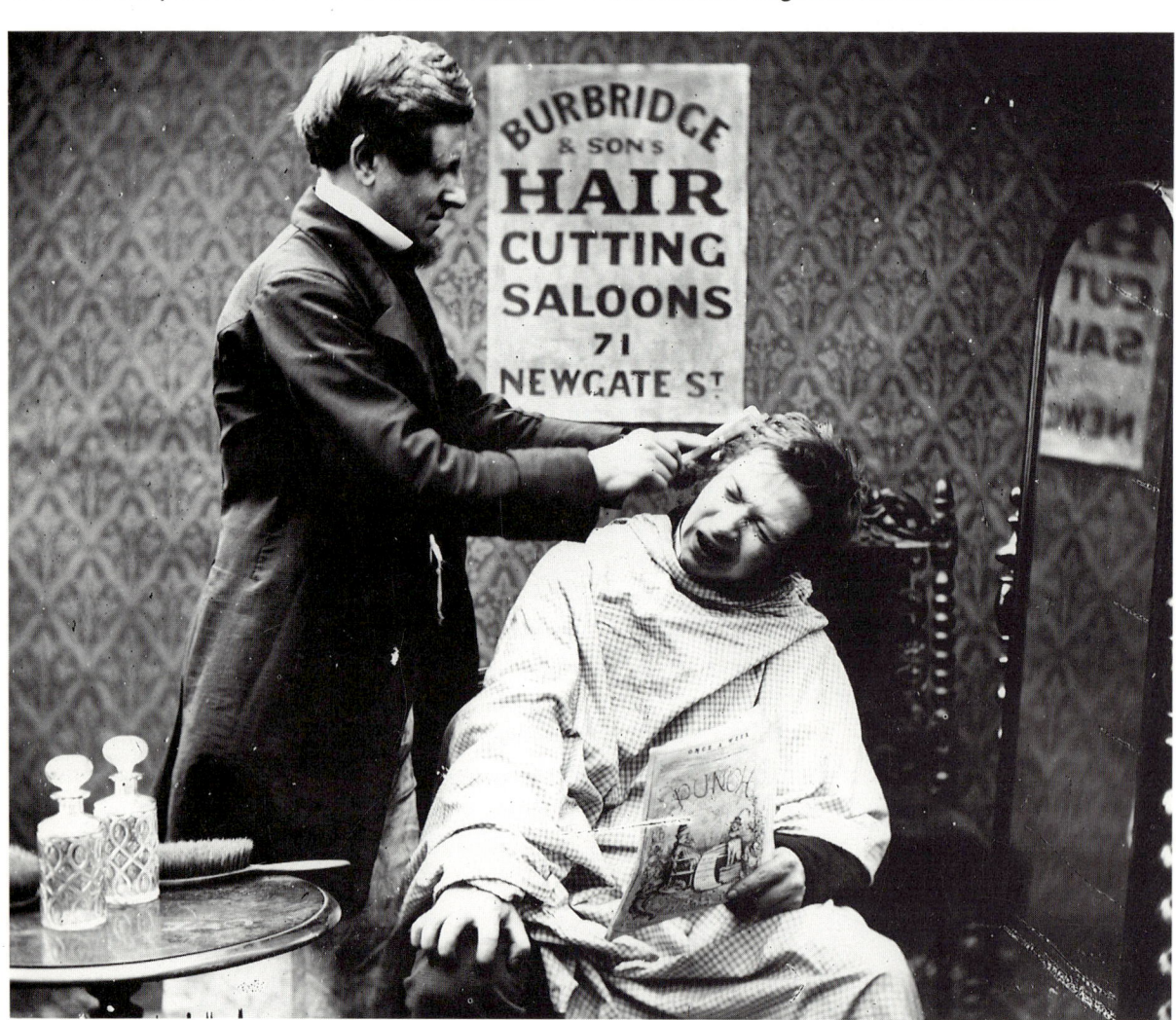

THE
Gentleman's Journal
And Youth's Miscellany
OF LITERATURE INFORMATION & AMUSEMENT

"I WANT THE POWER TO KILL HIM—TO HUNT HIM TO DEATH!" EXCLAIMED ALEC.

LITTLE JEM & JACK DIGGORY.
BY THE AUTHOR OF "THE PILOT BOY," "ELLA ST. MAUR," ETC.

witnessed by Jem. The poor child had scarcely time to utter a cry, or cast one look back, before he was rolled up in a huge cloak, or blanket, and roughly deposited at the bottom of the

The ruffians who had thus somewhat mysteriously carried off Jem, imagined, most fondly, that his cries would soon cease; but for once their imagination was most erroneous.

In the eighteenth century, magazines covered not only leisure interests but also political and religious issues. In North America, the *Pennsylvanian Magazine* ran articles by a British immigrant called Tom Paine arguing for American independence from Britain. The British government recognized the power of the press to influence public opinion and made strenuous efforts to control the printed word. Criminal proceedings were taken against individuals for printing what were considered to be 'unfitting wordes' criticizing the government. By 1765 a British Parliament Act imposed a stamp duty on every printed sheet and a tax on advertisements appearing in newspapers in Britain and its American colonies. This caused considerable resentment in America and added to the conflict that eventually resulted in the American War of Independence.

Despite efforts to control the press, the number of printers continued to grow and production became easier with new technical developments. The hand-operated wooden

Below *Mobile news-stands were introduced in 1950. They were popular with travellers.*

Above *Tom Paine, editor of one of America's earliest magazines,* The Pennsylvanian Magazine.

Newspaper and magazine vendors can still be found competing for the attention of the customer, as they did here.

printing press gave way to the steam-driven cylinder press, which was faster and cheaper. Inventions in type composition, the manufacture of wood pulp paper and new, quick-drying inks improved the quality of publications. The distribution of magazines and newspapers became swifter with the introduction of the new steam trains. In Britain, W.H. Smith's Book Company sold publications at news-stands in the new, crowded railway stations. American distribution agencies followed the British example and set up roadside news-stands following the so-called 'London plan'. Vendors were paid bonuses according to the number of copies sold. The customers were attracted by loud cries, which vendors still make on street corners today.

During the nineteenth century a number of important parliamentary acts were passed in Britain, setting up free education for all by the end of the century. Likewise, state schools and universities sprang up all over the USA. A new reading public emerged who could not afford books but who wanted cheap reading matter. Magazines provided the answer and their circulations rose as a result of the increased demand. In the face of this steady growth, the last state controls of the press at this time were removed. The withdrawal of taxes on publications, paper and advertisements meant that the printing industry was now free to expand.

Popular magazine journalism started in the USA. Enterprising publishers found that a combination of stories, lively news coverage and, later, photographs provided the right ingredients for the readers of cheap magazines such as *Munsey's* and *McClures.* These

magazines, which took their names from their owners, sold in millions. At the same time women's magazines such as *Ladies Home Journal* appeared on the magazine racks. These featured recipes, dress patterns and problem pages. Cheap fiction magazines such as *Romantic Confessions* also became popular.

The idea caught on in Britain and several all-fiction weeklies were launched which became known as 'penny dreadfuls'. Likewise cheap and cheerful general interest magazines such as *Answers, Titbits* and *Pearson's Weekly* became bestsellers too. Alfred Harmsworth (later Lord Northcliffe) who published *Answers* used his profits to start more magazines such as *Home Chat* for women as well as *Comic Cuts* by the 1890s. By extending the formula of light entertainment to daily newspapers, he went on to found the *Daily Mail* and the *Daily Mirror,* incorporating the ever-popular comic strips.

Mass production methods were needed to meet the demand for the new general weeklies, and so the magazine industry was born. Magazines such as Titbits *and* Pearson's Weekly *proved to be very popular.*

By the turn of the century magazines had become big business. Advertising was the key to this success. Manufacturers needed to market their products and in the days before television and radio, magazines were the ideal place for publicity. In turn, magazines became financially dependent on advertising. To encourage this partnership, magazines such as *Good Housekeeping* provided their readers with consumer advice on the new products in the shops alongside advertisements for the same items. These magazines were known as 'service' guides because they provided practical help for the reader as well as entertainment.

By the 1920s and 1930s, the old magazines had become dull and predictable and were overtaken by new publications with new formulas. The *Reader's Digest* in the USA recycled old magazines by editing articles into shorter versions called 'digests'. In time this grew into a major business operation with a record and book club and international editions in Britain and Australia. *Negro Digest* adapted

News magazines Time *and* Newsweek *provide the USA's answer to British national daily newspapers.*

the successful formula for a black audience in the USA and other black magazines like *Ebony* and the weekly newspaper *Jet* followed a few years later.

In the USA news magazines like *Time* and *Newsweek* provided weekly summaries of world events gathered from their information bureaux across the world. At the same time, widespread public interest in newsreel films and newspaper photography led publishers to start a new kind of photo-magazine. *Life* magazine combined high quality photographs with a minimum of words and proved so successful that it was soon copied by the *Picture Post* in Britain. By the 1960s *Time* was sold world-wide and had become a multinational company with interests in radio, television, book publishing and mail-order services. During these years of expansion, fortunes were made and small magazine companies grew into publishing empires.

New magazines were devoted to the world of film and television. The cartoon characters Tom and Jerry appeared in the pages of TV Comic.

After the Second World War the magazine industry expanded rapidly. The publication of trade, technical and professional magazines increased with the expansion of the economy in the post-war years. Although not always visible on the news-stand, they multiplied fast covering every possible area of employment until by the 1970s the giant British publishing company IPC was printing over 60 business publications alone. No area of work was neglected, from management to nursing. There was even an American magazine called *Ice Cream Field* providing news, views and 'how-to' information for readers in the confectionery business.

The arrival of television alongside radio and newspapers had a considerable effect on both magazines and comics. Magazine publishers found themselves competing for the same advertisers and audiences as the electronic media. Up-to-date news on radio and television forced newspapers to cover background stories previously covered only by the magazine sector. General-interest magazine circulation dropped and in the search for new readers these titles gave way to special-interest magazines. Magazines have had to learn how to exploit the popularity of television with the rise of television

listings magazines providing weekly programme information. Many magazines now have regular articles on television personalities and there are also publications on television soap operas as well as comics based on television cartoons.

Television companies now transmit electronic magazine channels. The numbered pages may be 'turned' by a control button and the pages provide news, weather and business information as well as general-interest items like recipes and sports results. Likewise, the video world is ready for developments in magazine publishing. Already there are some well established video magazines such as *Retailing World* for the grocery trade or *Practice* for vets. The visual advantages of video over print have helped it to develop in the medical professions in which filmed demonstrations can keep doctors up-to-date with the latest surgical developments. These video magazines may well point to the shape of things to come in the future.

2 How the industry works

Today there are a large number of comic and magazine publishers spread throughout the world, but the industry is dominated by a small group of multinational companies. Among the biggest are IPC, the National Magazine Company and the International Thomson Organization. These companies are part of larger businesses called conglomerates. They operate internationally and are often involved in a wide range of interests, from television to oil exploration, which bring in enormous profits for their parent companies.

These companies print thousands of comics and magazines every year. Most are published either weekly or monthly. Some are quarterly journals and others appear at less regular intervals. There are basically two categories of publications — consumer comics and magazines and trade, technical and professional magazines known simply as trade magazines. Consumer magazines are available on the news-stand for the general public and include women's magazines, current affairs journals, home-entertainment guides and children's comics. The trade magazines greatly outnumber the consumer titles but often have much smaller circulations and provide specialized news and information about the industry, profession or trade they serve. There is even a magazine called *Inky Fingers* for the small army of newspaper delivery boys and girls in Britain.

A company may own several titles but each magazine has its own publisher who is responsible for the overall business organization. The editors oversee the different stages of production and control the content. They rely on their ability to understand the magazine's readers by recognizing their interests, tastes and worries and by attempting to stay one step ahead. In order to do this the editors must keep in close contact with their readers, respond to letters and carry out reader surveys and questionnaires.

The magazine's editor depends on advice and contributions from members of the editorial team when deciding what to publish.

Although different editors work in different ways, they all follow the same basic procedure. Planning discussions take place with their editorial team and the articles are written by writers to an agreed formula, often months in advance of publication. Items such as film reviews are left to the last moment to keep them topical. Then the art editor designs the layout of the magazine. Photographs and pictures are incorporated on the page alongside the articles and their titles in an attractive easy-to-read style. Finally the magazine is sent to the printers.

In recent years, computer technology has revolutionized magazine production. Computerized publishing systems now allow magazine layouts to be compiled directly on the computer screen rather than by the slow method of cutting up and pasting down pages by hand. Typesetting can be done on the same machinery which also speeds up the process. Soon computer graphics will be able to

Left *The design of the magazine's cover is important because this is what the customer may judge it by.*

Below *Computerized publishing systems allow for last minute changes to the magazine.*

reproduce hand-drawn comic characters and simply place them on different backgrounds taken from the computer memory. Complete magazine publications can be transported across the world in seconds for international publication by facsimile electronic communications systems (fax).

The advertising department of a magazine is as important as the editorial side. Magazine sales provide only part of the income for a magazine. The other part comes from advertisers who pay to display advertisements for their products on the page to attract the attention of the reader. Approximately half of an average magazine is taken up by advertisements which add colour and variety as well as increasing the total number of pages. Advertisers are continually trying to find exciting ways to catch the reader's attention. They use small insert booklets, free records and free

Publishers increase their sales figures when free gifts are given away with the magazine.

samples. In most magazines, the amount of advertising dictates how many pages there will be in an issue.

It is the job of the advertising sales representative to persuade advertisers to use their particular magazine. They try to convince the advertisers that their product will be seen by the maximum number of people in the target audience (i.e. those expected to be interested in the product and have the money to buy it). To persuade the advertisers, the sales representative must know what kind of person reads the magazine. Are they young or old? Male or female? Single or married? This kind of information is provided by continuous readership research from organizations such as Britain's National Readership Survey.

Wholesalers have for many years distributed newspapers and magazines to retailers around the clock seven days a week.

Once the editorial and advertising sections are compiled, the magazine is sent to the printers. After printing, the next step is to get the magazine to the readers, a process known as distribution. There are several different methods of distributing comics and magazines. In the USA most magazines are distributed through supermarket stores or sold by subscription charge, with the magazine being sent through the post to the customer. In Britain the majority of trade magazines are also distributed through the post. Most of the large magazine publishing companies have their own distribution companies to deliver the comics and magazines by rail, road or air to the shops. Smaller publishers have to rely on wholesale companies who buy in bulk from the publishers who in turn distribute to the shops. These shops are known in the trade as retail outlets and sell directly to the customer. There are over 50,000 shops, newsagents and kiosks across Britain alone and many of these employ

Above *Large companies own chains of newsagents, but individual vendor's stalls are still very popular.*

Below *Open street dispensers provide an effective method of distributing free magazines to the public.*

boys and girls for home deliveries, so distribution is a highly complex operation to co-ordinate. The retailers collect the cover price from the customer and after taking a portion for themselves and giving a portion to the wholesaler, the magazine publisher may receive 50 per cent or less of the price on the front cover.

Free magazines are financed entirely by advertising. They are distributed door-to-door, handed out to passers-by on the street, placed in hotel rooms, aeroplane seats or put in street dispensers for passers-by to pick up. The delivery of these magazines in a particular area is known as 'rifle' distribution, because it is carefully targeted and aimed at a particular audience. *LAM* (London's Australasian Magazine) for instance, is packed full of travel advertisements for flights to Australia. It is available free in street dispensers in areas of London popular with Australasian visitors. Some churches also circulate free magazines. *The Plain Truth* is a magazine supported by US-based Fundamentalist Church, who distribute seven million free copies each month.

Alongside the major international publishing companies, there are numerous smaller ones such as the German group Grüner and Jahr who have translated their most successful titles such as *Prima* for the British market. Other smaller companies like EMAP, Argus and Ratepress have all developed specialist magazine markets by discovering new audiences previously not catered for by the publishing giants. The black publishing company, Ratepress, has developed glossy magazines for black people in Britain such as *Chic* and *Black Beat* as well as the successful

Chic is Britain's first black women's glossy magazine. It is set to become as popular as its American sister publication, Essence.

newspaper *The Voice*. The larger companies watch the progress of these new magazines and quickly bring out imitations if they prove to be successful. Whether or not these magazines are successful, they are breaking new ground by reaching new audiences and experimenting with new designs and magazine styles, so providing an ever expanding range from which the reader can choose.

3 Comics and Teenage Magazines

Comics are part of the universal experience of children today — but this was not always so. The first comics were aimed primarily at adults. Pull-out sections from newspapers, combining pictures, jokes and stories proved to be successful and they soon became publications in their own right. Since these early comics were printed on cheap paper, the picture quality was not very clear. In order to overcome this problem, the British cartoonist, Tom Brown, devised a style of bold, black lines and simple shapes in *Illustrated Chips* in the late nineteenth century. This proved to be very effective and this style continues to this day.

In the USA, fierce competition between the popular newspapers encouraged the development of colour supplements called 'funnies'. Next to sensational headlines, comic strips proved to be the most effective sales gimmick and a strip called *The Yellow Kid* improved the popularity of the Sunday edition of the *New York World.* Soon the daily strip came into existence when the comic characters *Mutt and Jeff* met for the first time on the pages of a newspaper and predicted 'This is gonna be a scream!'

Many of today's comic conventions were established at this time. Colourful words suggested sounds, such as 'POW' and 'ZAP'. Thoughts and words were expressed in speech balloons rather than captions and a series of lines on the cartoon conveyed a sense of movement. There were also frames enclosing each picture and the words 'to be continued . . .' at the end of the strip. Popular themes such as tramps, police, gangs of mischievous youngsters and funny little animals with human characteristics soon became established as firm favourites in cartoon strips.

The new comic form was employed in a variety of ways. The educational comic *Chick's Own* appeared using Stri-pey the Ti-ger, in which all words of more than one syllable were hyphenated to help children to learn to read and write. Commercial companies soon caught on to the potential of using comic characters to sell their products. In Britain the Ovaltine drink manufacturers created the Ovaltineys, who had their own comic. In the USA, Buster Brown sold everything from toys to cigars.

From the early days, film supplied comics with a wealth of material. Both Charlie Chaplin and Mickey Mouse were recast in comics throughout the world and in time *Film Fun, Radio Fun* and *TV Comic* all carried stories about established media stars and personalities. In the British *Film Fun* Laurel and Hardy became British citizens and the height of

Publishers discovered a lucrative market in children's publications. Now every member of the family could have their own reading matter.

First published in 1920, *Film Fun based all its comic strips on real film comedians. Regular stories such as 'Laurel and Hardy' were popular for years.*

their ambition was to have a slap-up feed of sausage and mash at the 'Hotel de Posh'.

As comics and cartoon strips became increasingly popular the demand for new material outstripped the number of cartoons available. To cater for this growing market, syndication agencies such as King Features developed in the USA. Using established newspaper distribution networks, a group of publishers would form a syndicate. The syndicate sold the reprint rights of the cartoon strip for simultaneous publication by a number of newspapers and magazines all over the world. Another way to sell these comic strips was to reprint serials from weekly newspapers into books or 'libraries'. Complete *Mutt and Jeff* comic strips were sent out on receipt of coupons as a special sales gimmick for the *Chicago America* as early as 1911. The new format caught on and was quickly imitated, with collections of well-loved strips such as *Little*

Orphan Annie in the USA and the famous schoolboy saga of Billy Bunter in *The Magnet* Library in Britain.

Adventure strip characters were the forerunners of the superhero comics. In 1938 *Superman* first appeared in Action Comics and his success gave rise to a whole battalion of superheroes such as *Batman* and *Captain Marvel*. These superheroes had their female counterparts, too, in the form of *Marvel Girl, Batgirl* and *Wonderwoman*. Produced to a basic formula, each hero had a secret identity and superhuman qualities. Often accompanied by a junior partner, they fought on the side of good against evil and dispensed instant justice to the super-villains. When they first appeared these heroes struggled against natural catastrophes;

during the Second World War, they took on U-boats and battleships and as a consequence they became war heroes.

The Second World War brought paper rationing, which reduced the number of pages and the availability of comics on the news-stands. Those comic characters that survived joined the army and contributed to the war effort. In the USA *Captain Easy* caught spies on the home front. The British comic character *Jane* became the British forces pin-up and *Bluey and Curley* played their part in Australia. In fact long after the war had ended the conflict continued to be fought in the pages of the comics. In Australia the comic strip heroine 'Jane' was so popular that she was even awarded her own comic paper.

In the aftermath of the war, the antics of the adventure strip heroes started to seem unreal against the true horror of the conflict. The novelty had worn thin and the comic industry went into a decline. In an effort to bolster sales, publishers turned to more and more extreme crime and horror stories aimed at adults but often read by young people. There was a public outcry by parents on both sides of the Atlantic, who feared the corruption of their children. In 1954 the US Senate held investigations into these comics, and to fend off the threat of censorship, the industry established a comics code authority to lay down guidelines regarding the content of comics. In Britain, a similar campaign led to the 1955 Children and Young Person's Harmful Publications Act, which is still in force today.

Heroes in these comics must be invincible god-like creatures who are far superior to any human being.

Meanwhile in Britain during the 1950s, the Reverend M. Morris launched one of the most successful boys' comics, *Eagle,* starring 'Dan Dare — the intrepid space Colonel'. Attempting to give a moral perspective based on Christian values, *Eagle* was not just a comic but a club in which readers could participate. Readers' activities included carol services, exhibitions and *Eagle* club holidays. Television cartoon series characters injected new life into these children's comics too. American superheroes joined forces to form *The Fantastic Four* fighting ever more evil adversaries such as 'Mahkizmo — the Nuclear Man', and the first black superhero appeared called 'The Black Panther'. In the adult world, people's hopes and fears found expression in thoughtful newspaper strips such as *Doonesbury* and *Peanuts.*

In Britain the publishers D.C. Thomson produced Britain's most popular comics. *The Dandy* is the longest running comic, featuring 'Desperate Dan' — the Cactusville hero who munches on cow pies. *The Beano* is still also a best seller (selling around 600,000 copies per week at the peak of its popularity) and is packed

Above *Hulton Press published* Eagle *with the aim of raising general standards of quality. It was launched with an advertising campaign aimed at parents.*

Above right *The* Dandy *started as an 8-page pull-out section in the British newspaper the* Sunday Post.

Below right *Comic superheroes like Superman are used by advertisers to convey messages to the young.*

full of riotous characters such as 'The Bash Street Kids' and 'Roger the Dodger' a character who is always up to no good and gets a good whacking in the end. However, in recent years there has been an overall decline in the sale of children's comics. Television and film have taken over the comic art form. In order to survive, new comics have to be launched with tie-in products from the toy industry, backed with film or television series such as *Action Force* in Britain and the US version *G.I. Joe* as well as *The Care Bears* for young readers. Even *Superman* has been hired by the British Health Education Council to advise against smoking cigarettes.

Comics and magazines are still very popular with teenagers. They can provide hours of endless fun away from the world of adults. However, comics and magazines for teenagers are clearly divided into boys' and girls' magazines. Photo-story magazines which focus on romance, fashion and beauty are aimed at girls. Picture story comics or special interest magazines for hobbies tend to be read more by boys.

Action-packed adventure stories are usually read by boys in their early teens and perhaps the most popular setting for these dramas is the sports field. In Britain *Shoot* and *Roy of the Rovers* have feature articles on famous soccer players and comic strip heroes who combine team spirit with individual star performances to overcome all obstacles, week after week. These

Above *Boys continue to enjoy reading comics well into their teens. Collecting these comics has become a popular pastime.*

Below *The girls' publishing market begins with comics and ends with glossy women's magazines. In between are photo-stories for teenagers.*

sorts of heroes are also found in war comics such as *Battle With Stormforce*. Team colours are swapped for combat uniform, but essentially the heroes remain the same — men with square, determined jaw lines and strong, muscle-bound bodies. Often known by nicknames such as 'Johnny Red', they fight on the side of right against might and usually win in the end. War comics are printed in library-sized booklets containing a single complete story in the USA. Weekly comics with several serial stories are sold in Britain and Australia. At the start of each story, the time and place is set such as '1942 — The Stalingrad Battle Zone', but the stories are usually told from the British or American point of view. The cast of characters is almost always white and there is no mention of the contribution of West Indian, African or Asian soldiers to these wars. This is surprising since these stories are otherwise written with careful attention to historical details. Aircraft model numbers and popular wartime

Popular football hero Roy of the Rovers now stars in his own comic.

slang give the stories the all-important touch of reality that readers enjoy so much.

War comics give way to the more popular science-fiction adventures in the older teenage market. In Britain and Australia, the award winning *2000 AD* is billed as the galaxy's greatest comic. It has a particular brand of tongue-in-cheek humour directed at everything from girls' photo-romance magazines to the British royal family. Set in the future world, the comic is full of mutant heroes — half-human, half-beast, descended from the Superman tradition of Marvel comics in the USA. The star of the comic is the violent 'Judge Dredd', a detective who inhabits the future world's 'Mega city' in his own series. The character has proved so popular that his adventures are reprinted in monthlies, albums, specials and now a full-length feature film.

When boys grow out of their comics, there is no special group of magazines for them to read if they are interested in fashion or how to get on with girls. Instead there are a multitude of publications for special interests which may appeal mainly to boys, such as *Motorcycle News.* By complete contrast girls' comics and, later magazines are available for all age groups. The British comics such as *Bunty* and *Debbie* carry stories about girls who love animals and have ambitions to become famous dancers. Then girls graduate on to teenage magazines such as *My Guy* and *Patches.* These magazines contain black and white photo-stories in the style of the Italian *fumetti* libraries. Interests and ambitions fall by the wayside in favour of beauty and fashion and the central aim of 'getting and keeping a man'.

Romance underpins every article in teenage girls' magazines and even pop music features concentrate more on the performers themselves than on their music. Handsome male 'hunks' are displayed on the front covers, back pages and in the centre-page pin-up, so readers can stick them on to their bedroom

Girls are encouraged to 'improve' themselves through the fashion and beauty pages of magazines.

Every girls' magazine has a problem page which provides an advice service to readers.

walls to weave into romantic daydreams. These images are backed up with interviews with the stars which are designed to show that the idols are really just like the ordinary boy-next-door. Interview questions such as 'How many Valentine cards do you normally send?' encourage readers' romantic notions.

While most teenage magazines are being constantly updated to keep up with the latest trends, one feature remains the same. The problem page concentrates on the realities of day-to-day life in contrast to the photo-stories. The letters filling these pages are often of a highly personal nature concerning relationships and health issues. Boys' magazines do not provide this service and sometimes boys write to girls' magazines problem pages. In Britain, *Jackie* has recognized this and made efforts to include boys in the magazine. This indicates that boys and girls share more common interests than the traditional teenage magazines would suggest.

At the older end of the teenage market, *Love Affair* and *Photolove* have cuddling couples on their front covers and continue the single-minded obsession with romance. The photo-strip pictures remain the same but these stories deal with the problems of newly-married couples and caring for young children. As generations of teenagers grow up, the magazine market continually strives to keep up with them. Recently British publishers have come up with bright and newsy magazines such as *Mizz, Just Seventeen* and *FSM* (Fairly Serious Monthly) which aim to cover a wider range of issues affecting young people today. Publishers are always eager to woo the teenager magazine market because as young people grow into adulthood, they are likely to continue the habit of buying magazines formed at this age.

4 Music magazines and the Alternative Press

Fifty years ago the first music paper began to cover the fashionable jazz-music scene. By the 1960s when Elvis Presley and The Beatles were world-famous, pop music was adopted by the media. Increasing amounts of air time were devoted to music on television, radio and cable television channels as audience ratings soared. Likewise, the magazine industry discovered a new group of young people eager for information about their favourite singers and bands. This swelling tide of interest has encouraged the publication of an ever-expanding range of magazines to suit all musical tastes.

In the 1960s an American student called Jann Wenner 'dropped out' of university and started a twice-monthly rock and roll music paper called *Rolling Stone.* It combined a mixture of current affairs and celebrity interviews with coverage of music. The root of *Rolling Stone*'s popularity lay in a new journalistic style in which the writers wrote more about themselves than the subject they were covering (a style known as 'new journalism'). *Rolling Stone* gradually grew from an underground student paper into the most successful music magazine in the country. However, as time passed, *Rolling Stone*'s readers grew older and were no longer just interested in music, so the magazine changed to cover cultural events and current affairs.

Music magazines provide a running commentary on the music industry as a whole. In return they rely on the music business for advertising revenue.

Eventually an off-shoot magazine, called *Record,* was launched devoted entirely to music, catering for a new generation of music fans. Youth-culture magazines have always succeeded or failed according to how well they have been in tune with the current trends in music.

Music publications are designed along the same lines as 'tabloid' newspapers. They became popular throughout the world and were quickly imitated, with the publication of *Creem* and *Ram* in Australia. In Britain the tabloid *Melody Maker* developed a reputation as the 'musician's paper', because of its classified advertisements section in which readers could sell their instruments and advertise for 'Musicians Wanted'. Internationally famous pop groups such as The Police and Duran Duran have all met through the pages of *Melody Maker.*

Music magazines must be swift to respond to new musical trends, otherwise they can quickly become out of date.

In the 1970s the British magazine *New Musical Express (NME)* repeated *Rolling Stone*'s tabloid formula and sold well in both Australia and Britain. With a mixture of music, media and politics, it soon became Britain's leading youth paper. By the late 1970s when punk music exploded on to the scene *NME* had to change its style. In order to do this, brash and exciting new writers were brought on to the paper, recruited straight from the magazine's readership. In response to a small advertisement in the paper which read 'Wanted: hip young gun slingers', young readers like Julie Birchill became *NME* reporters overnight and guided the magazine through the punk years.

27

At this time several young readers became writers themselves because they felt the mainstream music papers were not in touch with the independent record label music. They turned their backs on the mainstream press and wrote their own magazines, which became known as 'fanzines' (short for fan magazines). These home-made magazines were typed by hand, photocopied and distributed at concerts or by subscription through the post. Despite their shabby appearance, the basic message shared by all the fanzines is that anyone can join in either by writing articles, taking photographs or even drawing cartoons.

Today these fanzines are produced throughout Britain, the USA and Australia but largely on a local basis. They vary enormously from the British *A New England* which combines an interest in music and football to the more sophisticated *House of Dolls* which has its own cartoon and 'gig' listings in both its British and American editions. The inventiveness of the fanzines has been recognized by the mainstream press who keep a watchful eye on them and often employ promising young writers on their national magazines.

To date, the most popular music magazines are the 'glossies' — so called because of the shiny paper they are printed on. There is a *Smash Hits* in Britain and Australia and a sister publication in the USA called *Star Hits,* catering for a younger age range. Produced in a smaller magazine-type format, they combine song lyrics and colour posters with pop star interviews and articles on chart music. In order for these top-selling magazines to maintain their popularity they need to develop a good

Do-it-yourself magazines for the alternative pop music scene. Fanzine writers pride themselves on their home-spun image.

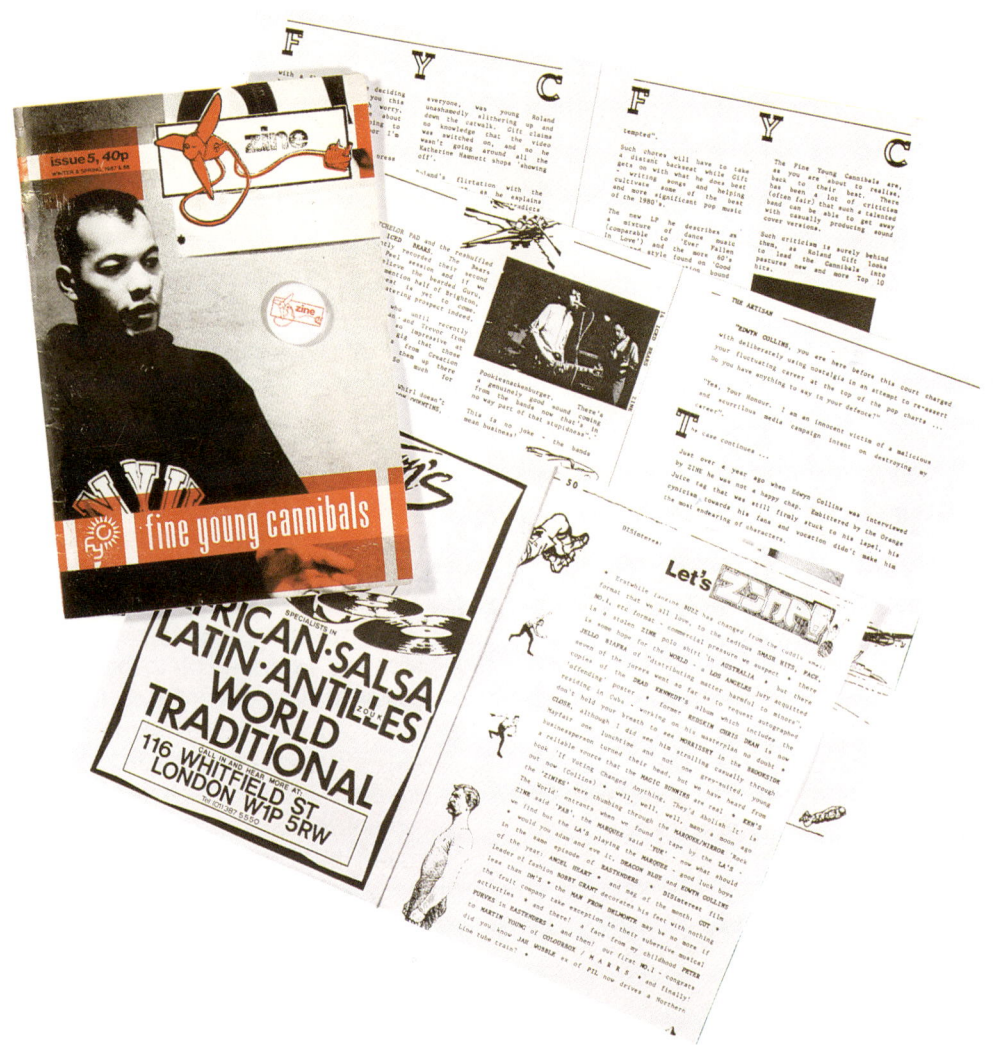

understanding of their readers. Questionnaires in the magazine, the reader's letters' page, pen-friend ads and fan club information services allow the editor to determine which are currently the most popular groups with their readers.

Information about the readers is also important for the companies who wish to advertise in the magazines. The music industry itself provides the bulk of the advertising. Advertisements for new releases on record, cassette or CD, together with the magazine's reviews draw valuable attention to new bands and artists. Besides this, all kinds of items are promoted in the teenage 'glossies' from soft drinks to wrist-watches. Free thin vinyl records are sometimes given away telling the readers about such things as bank accounts for young people. The advertisers know that it is important to attract young readers because the teenagers of today will be the bank-account holders of tomorrow. Advertising competition is very intense in this sector of the market.

At the beginning of the 1980s, lifestyle

New publications continue to arrive on the market for a new generation of teenagers, while some old ones keep changing to stay ahead.

'glossies' for the older age range came on to the market in Britain in the form of *The Face, Blitz, ID* and *Sky.* These magazines are not just concerned with the latest trends in music, they also pride themselves on documenting up-to-the-minute fashion in everything from hair-styles to hi-fi equipment. The message they give is 'it's not what you say but the way that you look that counts.' This concern with style has extended to the presentation of the magazine. They have experimented with design, type and graphics by breaking all the traditional rules of magazine layout. Nick Logan, the pioneering editor of *The Face* described how. 'One month we squashed all the headlines as they came off the typesetter. The next week every pop paper in town was doing it.' However, fashion is constantly changing, and these magazines have to change with it.

Between the tabloids and the glossies, there are a whole host of specialist titles reflecting an incredible variety of musical tastes from *Wire*, the British Jazz magazine to *Kerrang!*, which is entirely devoted to 'heavy metal' music. The success of this magazine led to the promotion of *Kerrang!* as a brand name. There is a *Kerrang!* video and album, and new bi-monthly magazine called *Extra-Kerrang!* and even a magazine written entirely by its readers called *Kerrang Kontaktz*. As the magazine publisher says, 'Anything under the 'Kerrang' banner will sell!'

Perhaps the most interesting development in music publications are the new free magazines.

Free music magazines have proved very successful with advertisers because they reach the record-buying audience in the stores.

Financed entirely by advertising, these magazines are given away to all customers at the large music shops in both Britain and the USA. Tower record shops have a free magazine called *Pulse,* and a British twin called *Top*. The retail company produces the magazine, which has been an instant success in marketing terms because it is distributed directly to the record-buying audience. As the music press becomes more and more specialized, this kind of magazine may become increasingly popular.

5 Women's magazines

Women's magazines have influenced generations of women. *The Ladies' Mercury,* published in 1693, was one of the earliest magazines. It combined snippets of news from home and abroad with articles on home management and fiction. The contents of these early magazines were well meaning but rather dull and reflected the editor's views on how a young woman should behave. The editor of *The Ladies' Diary* determined that his magazine should advise his readers: 'What all young women ought to be — innocent, modest, instructive and agreeable'.

The first women's magazines were published annually. They contained a calendar and snippets of information together with puzzles and poetry.

THE YOUNG LADIES' JOURNAL

AN ILLUSTRATED MAGAZINE

COSSIE WAS IN HIGH SPIRITS THIS EVENING.

ONLY A HEART.

BY THE AUTHOR OF "SPENSER'S WIFE," "PAUL
DEVRON'S LEGACY," "A TWISTED LINK," "CLASPED
WITH RUBIES," "DUKE WYNNE'S DAUGHTERS," ETC.

CHAPTER XXII.

A PERPLEXING CIRCUMSTANCE.

her the cup of tea which he thought most likely
to prove an acceptable restorative. At first May
felt unable to swallow it, but when he so kindly
pressed it upon her that further refusal sounded
ungrateful, she made the effort. Then, as he
saw her more capable of listening to him, he sat
down beside her, and talked, not of the present,
but of that future in which she had also her
"You shake your head. Just at this minute it
seems an interminable period, but it will slip by
so rapidly, that you will wake some morning and
find it—gone. Besides, in a little while, you will
have wiped away these tears at parting, and be
picturing to yourself what you shall say, and how
your husband will look, when he is restored to

This tradition of self-help and improvement continued into the nineteenth century. By this time developments in printing technology and improvements in the railway distribution services made magazines more easily available. The increasing numbers of people who could read also contributed to the growth of the women's press. Titles more than doubled between 1875 and 1900 in Britain alone. There was a new audience of working women reading the all-fiction weeklies with smart titles like *My Lady's Novelette*. This new magazine industry was supported by manufacturers who realized they could advertise their products in magazines read by a new female audience who had their own money to spend.

At the turn of the century many new magazines came on to the market such as *Home Chat* in Britain and *Woman's Home Companion* in the USA. The demand continued to grow and American monthlies like *Vogue* and *Good Housekeeping* were transported on to the British market too. *Good Housekeeping* was one of the early 'service' magazines which devised recipes and ran 'shopping lists' of consumer items recommended by the magazine. They also tested gadgets on behalf of their readers. If passed, manufacturers were awarded a seal of guarantee as a mark of quality which many women learnt to trust as a guide on what to buy. Magazines and advertisers became increasingly reliant on one another to survive.

Although the Second World War resulted in paper rationing which reduced the size of women's magazines, the government recognized their importance as a channel of communication with the female population during this time of national crisis. Women's magazine editors regularly met government ministers and officials and translated government policies into practical advice in the magazine. They advised women how they could help in the war effort both at work and inside the home. There were suggestions on ways to save fuel, stretch food rations and how to keep their spirits up until the men came home from war. However, the magazines did not take notice of the real hardships that women were enduring, such as inadequate nursery provision for their children while they were doing their war work in factories.

When rationing came to an end, the war years gave way to a period of growth for magazines. Consumer goods started to flood on to the market and women needed help to choose from the range of labour-saving devices on offer. The magazines that had been women's war-time companions now became advisers on what to buy. Magazines in the USA such as *McCall's* and *Woman's Home Journal* became 'fireside shop windows' for busy women.

A token of regard & esteem from the Jones family

Every scrap of **METAL** is wanted — for guns and tanks and ships
Every scrap of **BONE** is wanted — for planes, explosives and fertilisers.
Every scrap of **PAPER** is wanted — for ammunition and other things.

By carefully putting out every bit of scrap metal, every bone and every scrap of paper, the Jones family have given the Government valuable defence material. They have rendered the country a very real service.

HELP TO WIN THE BATTLE OF BRITAIN AT YOUR OWN BACK-DOOR

"UP HOUSEWIVES AND AT 'EM!"

ISSUED BY THE MINISTRY OF SUPPLY

Left The Young Ladies' Journal *of the late nineteenth century encouraged advertising.*

Above *The British government was one of the largest magazine advertisers during the Second World War.*

In Britain, *Woman* became the best seller when printed in colour for the first time, mixing fiction with articles on fashion, furnishing and food. A new brand of story magazines and 'pocket libraries', such as *Romeo* and *Valentine,* came on to the market crammed full of romantic picture-strip stories and fiction for young married women and teenagers. The magazine industry had never had it so good.

The arrival of commercial television competing for the attentions of the advertisers badly affected the magazine industry. Mass women's weeklies went into a decline and the industry had to come up with new ideas to survive. One US magazine named *Family Circle* found a new method of distribution through the large supermarket stores. Picked up at the cash-till with the rest of the week's grocery shopping, it had no rivals and was an enormous success. The idea was transported over to Britain and was soon joined by a sister publication called *Living* for younger women. Today *Family Circle* is the best-selling women's magazine in both Britain and the USA.

Magazines had to find new clearly defined audiences to maintain their advertising revenue. The new 'teenager' had more money to spend and a new crop of magazines such as *Honey* in Britain and *Teen* in the USA became 'a girl's best friend' by advising them how to achieve their dreams. Now there are magazines devoted to a specific age group from *Seventeen* to *19* and *Over 21*.

Magazines in supermarkets are tailor-made to reach markets where 'housewife traffic' will be found.

The content of women's magazines varies from title to title, but they all share a common aim — to guide women on how to be 'better'. A basic formula has evolved which is shared by many of them. The first message is that it is important for a woman to strive always to keep young and beautiful. Pages are filled with fashion and beauty advice alongside advertisements for the items needed to fulfil this goal. There are also suggestions on how to improve home, health and career. To encourage readers to develop a sense of loyalty to one particular magazine month after month, each

Germaine Greer, one of the most well-known spokeswomen for women's liberation.

magazine carries its own quizzes, competitions, letters and problem pages as well as readers' guides to shopping. These activities all serve to involve readers in a club-like membership with the magazine.

During the 1960s, the Women's Liberation movement began to campaign to change women's role in society. The movement gave rise to new magazines like *MS* in the USA and *Spare Rib* in Britain as an alternative to the

Nowadays women work in all areas of industry and commerce and they want magazines that address work-related issues as well as traditional topics.

traditional women's publications. But it was not just the content of these magazines that was new. *Spare Rib* is totally independent of the big publishing companies which own most of the women's magazines in Britain. Its staff share all responsibilities collectively and are paid an equal wage. Existing on a shoe-string budget, it has consistently achieved strong circulations and played an important part in drawing women's issues to the attention of the public. By 1975 laws were passed in Britain on sexual discrimination and equal pay for women. These magazines continue to discuss women's rights issues.

The 'new woman' changed the profile of women's magazines. In Britain, *Nova* began to discuss a whole range of issues concerning the modern young woman, from the problems of living in a bedsit to new methods of contraception. At the same time in the USA

According to surveys, over half a million men read the British edition of Cosmopolitan *every month.*

there was a new type of magazine for the 'sexually liberated woman' called *Cosmopolitan* which was originally more concerned with good fun than with politics. The first issue contained a centre-page pin-up of a naked man and sold over a million copies. By 1982 there were 17 international editions across the world from Australia to Latin America. Today, women make up 40 per cent of the work-force so there are magazines to reflect this such as *Working Woman* found in both Britain and the USA.

These glossy magazines may be designed for women but at least 10 per cent of their readership is male. The advertising industry has recognized this 'hidden' audience and in the USA, Canada and Australia men have their own general-interest magazines such as *Gentleman's Quarterly.* Until recently this has not been the case in Britain. Strong national newspapers and special-interest magazines have limited the growth of men's magazines. The major women's magazines have tried to fill

this gap with supplements for men. *OM* in *Options* and *Man* in *Cosmopolitan* show how these publications have become magazines for couples, and advertisers can now 'target' both partners in the same magazine. These have proved popular and now there are men's fashion magazines on the market, such as *Arena*. However, they contain no articles on health issues and personal problems, issues that had attracted men to women's magazines in the first place.

Today, women's magazines are the largest single category of publications and more continue to arrive on the crowded display racks all the time. New and old magazines alike share the same basic preoccupations with showing their readers how to improve themselves. Yet these magazines also try to reflect the experience of women today.

6 Special-interest magazines

A survey of the magazine display shelves at the local news-stand will show that there is a large section loosely described as 'leisure interest'. Competition with television and newspapers has meant that many general-interest magazines have become a thing of the past. Now magazines are devoted to more specialized interests such as hobbies and pastimes. Magazines are targeted at specific audiences to maintain circulation figures and today this section contains something for everyone in the ever-changing leisure market.

In the age of television, the top-selling magazines across Europe and the USA are weekly listing publications such as the British *Radio Times* and *TV Times* and the American *TV Guide* which publish television programme information. These magazines have strong appeal with advertisers too as they are read continually throughout the week. In West Germany, there are nine weekly national television guides as well as numerous supplements, and even a special women's guide to television called *Bild-Woche*.

Sport is a leading leisure activity for participants and spectators alike and there are numerous publications devoted to it. Since British newspapers and television carry day-to-day bulletins on most sporting events, there are no general sporting magazines. Instead there are over 150 specialist individual sports titles from *Motorcycle News* to *Sub-Aqua Scene*. By contrast in Europe and the USA newspapers tend to be regional rather than national and carry regional sports news, and so the general sports magazines sell well. The best-selling

Massive television coverage of sports ensures that Sports Illustrated *is a popular American magazine.*

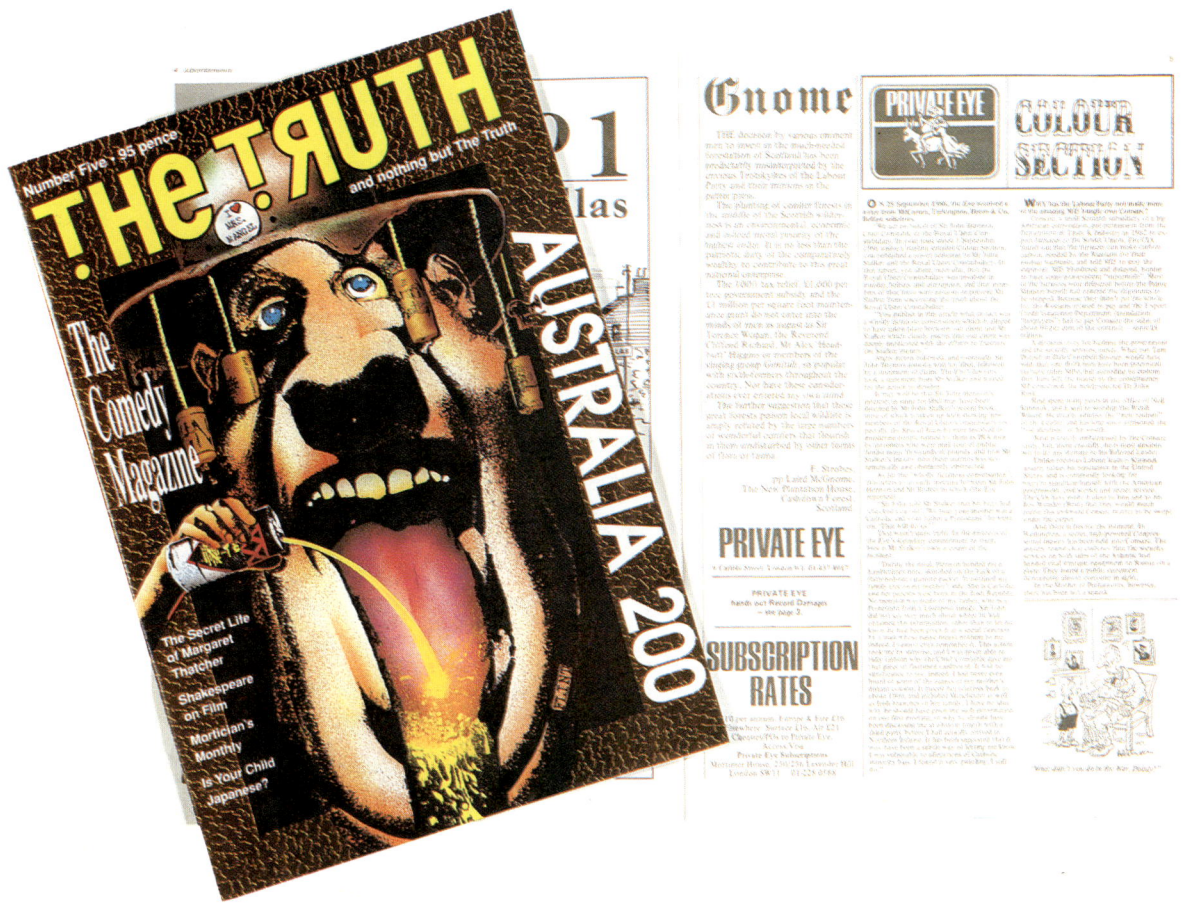

sports magazine in the USA is *Sports Illustrated*, combining vivid articles written from the players' point of view with superb photographs. Today *Sports Illustrated* boasts a readership of over 15 million people, most of whom are male.

The political and current affairs magazines appeal to those with a general interest in these matters and are collectively known as 'opinion-forming journals'. Many of these are long established, such as Britain's *The Economist, The New Statesman* and *The Spectator.* They are bought mainly by subscription. Circulations are currently in decline as a result of increased current affairs coverage in television programmes and in the daily newspapers. In the USA on the other hand, enormous distances from coast to coast prevent nationwide distribution of most newspapers. Instead news magazines such as *Time* and *Newsweek* provide weekly summaries of a wide

In Britain political satire is enjoying a revival in popularity. Now Private Eye *has been joined by several competing magazines.*

range of issues from international affairs to the arts, while *Business Week* concentrates on government and business news. On a less serious level, there is a magazine called *Private Eye* in Britain which contains humorous articles and cartoons on current affairs. It continues to survive despite frequently being taken to the law courts and fined large amounts of money because of its scandalous articles about well-known personalities and politicians.

Many people feel that the mainstream political magazines do not cater for their interests or print articles expressing their views. Black and other ethnic minority groups, feminists and gay people have solved this problem by producing their own magazines. *Gay News* is a publication for homosexuals and

Sunday newspapers and their magazines are designed to fit into the traditional lazy Sunday.

lesbians. *Sanity* is the British magazine for the Campaign for Nuclear Disarmament, a British pressure group. Both present alternative viewpoints and raise issues that may not be covered in the mainstream press. These kinds of magazines are either sold through their campaign group networks, by subscription or through bookshops and offer a broad range of opinions that would not otherwise be available.

The magazines run by Sunday newspapers as 'supplements' started in Britain in the 1960s in the 'quality' newspapers such as *The Sunday Times* and the *Observer*. They contained additional news features and articles and fulfilled a similar function to the general news magazines in the USA 'digesting' the news into one publication at the end of the week. These supplements were really just free magazines but had a unique method of distribution — they were slipped in between the pages of the parent newspapers. In recent years, they have included one-off specials or pulls-outs on popular subjects such as gardening, cookery or holidays. They carry advertisements for cars, alcohol and hi-fi equipment and are aimed primarily at a male audience relaxing at home over Sunday breakfast. The popular newspapers adopted the idea and now the *Mail on Sunday* has a separate magazine of its own called *You* with a pull-out cartoon section called *Biz*. Advertisers can now reach every member of the family in one publication.

Cartoon comics are popular with adults and children alike. As a result the comic industry is booming not just for the large companies such as D.C. Comics and Marvel, but also for the individual artists and writers who have a following both in Britain and the USA. They have become so popular that they are sold through 'direct sales' stores such as London's Forbidden Planet, which only sells comics.

Adults who grew up reading American super-hero comics now enjoy *2000 AD* and the punk comic *Love and Rockets.* There has been a revived interest in both old and new comics. Many people now collect them and there are international comic conferences, collector's fairs and associations of comic enthusiasts.

Love and Rockets marks a new wave of comics. It features two main stories of women's adventures which combine sadness and humour.

Devoted fans have their favourite comics and collect the work of particular artists such as Alan Moore, who uses the comic form in highly inventive ways. His story *Swamp Thing* and many others have also been highly successful in hardback publication.

The only publications directed at men alone are pornographic magazines which contain photographs of nude women in sexually explicit poses. One of the oldest is *Playboy,* which was first published in 1953. In time it became highly successful and broadened its scope beyond the centre-fold pin-up to include articles on fashion, travel, sports, cars and, of course, sex. The root of its success lay in its popularity with advertisers since it attracted an extremely large young male readership not reached by television. Imitations have sprung up such as

Above *Sailors look at pornographic magazines on sale. The market is a multi-million dollar industry.*

Right *Souvenir editions of London's* Evening Standard *commemorate a museum exhibition.*

Escape and *Penthouse* as well as many magazines with a more obscene content, and today the worldwide pornography industry is larger than the record and film industries combined.

There are some publications on the news-stand that are neither books nor magazines, but fall between these categories. Souvenir issues and one-off supplements are published on special occasions such as the British football Cup Finals or the Australian bicentenary, and they are sold as magazines on the news-stand.

Similarly there are 'partworks' which are slim booklets or loose-leaves bought in weekly instalments and collected into volumes or binders. They carry no advertising and so rely on massive promotional campaigns on television to raise enough interest so that readers will continue to buy them week-by-week until the series has been completed. There are often special offers on the set binders and the selling line 'Buy part one and get part two free' helps to launch these magazines on to the market.

Above *The local newsagent still provides an astounding choice of magazines each week.*

Today the magazine market is constantly changing. Thousands of new publications are printed every year to cash in on new areas of interest or hobbies and many of them will fail. Yet despite the threat of increasingly sophisticated electronic media, magazines will continue to survive because they provide such an enormous variety of entertainment, information and ideas for their readers.

Glossary

1955 Children and Young Person's Harmful Publications Act A law that states that it is illegal to publish, print or hire stories told in pictures (comics) portraying crimes, acts of violence or incidents of a repulsive or horrible nature which would corrupt a young person. It is still in force.

Circulation The number of magazines or comics sold each issue.

Conglomerate An industrial group made up of companies which often have different business interests and make enormous profits for the whole group.

Consumer magazines These publications may include most of the general interest magazines available for the general public on the news-stand including women's magazines, children's comics, home entertainment guides, pop music, leisure and current affairs magazines. The term also refers to the type of advertising these magazines carry. 'Consumer' advertisements encourage you to buy items for the home or for leisure interests as well as fashion and beauty products.

Digest A journal containing summary articles of the essential points from a particular news item or story.

Direct sale Shops that sell only a particular type of publication. This term is used when talking about specialist comic shops.

Editor The person with complete control over the contents of the publication and the future direction of the magazine.

Fanzine A home-made magazine compiled by an enthusiast — a fan magazine.

Facsimile (Fax) An exact 'electronic' copy of a document, which can be sent by a telephone line and reproduced in another location within seconds.

Feature A non-news article in a magazine or newspaper.

Glossy A magazine printed on shiny paper.

Layout The general appearance of a printed page designed by the art editor. Photographs and pictures are laid out with articles in an attractive and easy-to-read style.

Libraries Pocket-sized booklets which are published in a series to collect.

Partwork A magazine sold by instalments presented as parts of a book to form a whole series. They carry no advertising at all but are promoted by extensive television advertising with special offers on binders for the completed set.

Penny dreadful The popular name for the cheap penny magazines containing romantic or tear-jerking fiction. Penny dreadfuls were very popular with young working women in the nineteenth century.

Publisher The person responsible for the magazine's overall business organization within a company. It is the publisher's responsibility to ensure that the magazine is successful in terms of circulation and advertising as well as the smooth running of the departments in co-operation with one another.

Pulp magazines A cheap magazine originally printed on wood-pulp paper which contained sentimental and sensational stories and feature articles.

Retailer The newsagent who sells magazines and comics to the consumer.

Service magazines Publications which do not just entertain but offer a practical and useful service for the reader. They provide advice and information from experts.

Stamp Acts Eighteenth and nineteenth century British tax on newspapers and magazines to prevent the publication of articles critical of the government. The tax was set according to size, to raise the price and discourage readers from buying these publications, putting the publishers out of business.

Syndication A group of publishers who sell the reprint rights to articles or comic strips to be published by a number of newspapers and comics all around the world.

Tabloid A small format newspaper with an informal style and many photographs.

Tie-in The practice of launching a new comic alongside a toy, film or television series to maximise public awareness and profits from one comic.

Trade A short-hand description for trade, technical and professional magazines which provide news and information to educate and advise. Trade advertising concentrates on getting you interested in developments, products and jobs related to the work.

Typesetting To set (or type) the copy of the magazine for printing.

Wholesaler The group who buy the magazines and comics in large quantities from the publisher and distribute to the retailer.

Further Information

For further information on the issues covered in this book, please write to the following organizations:

Association of Comic Enthusiasts
80 Silverdale
London SE26 45J
Britain

Forbidden Planet (Science Fiction and Comic Bookshop)
23 Denmark Street
London WC2H 8NA
Britain

National Magazine Company Ltd.
National Magazine House
72 Broadwick Street
London W1V 2BP
Britain

Museum of Comic Art
Ward Castle, Comly Avenue
Rye, Porchester
New York 10573
USA

Rolling Stone
745 Fifth Avenue
New York, New York
10151 (21)
USA

Australian Magazine Publishers Association
St Andrews House
Sydney
New South Wales
Australia 2000

Booklist

Martin Barker *A Haunt of Fears: The Strange History of the British Horror Comics* (Pluto, 1984)
Dave Berry, Liz Cooper and Charles Landry *Where is the Other News? The News Trade and the Radical Press* (Minority Press Group, 1980)
Dave Berry, Liz Cooper and Charles Landry *The Other Secret Service: Press Distributors and Press Censorship* (Minority Press Group, 1980)
Edwin Emery and Michael Emery *The Press and America: An Interpretive History of the Mass Media* (Prentice Hall, 1984)
Marjorie Ferguson *Forever Feminine: Women's Magazines and the Cult of Femininity* (Heinemann, 1983)
Denis Gifford *The International Book of Comics* (Dean International, 1984)

John Hartley, Hooly Goulden and Tim O'Sullivan *Making Sense of the Media* (Comedia, 1985)
Judith Hemming and Jane Leggett *Comics and Magazines* (The English Centre, 1984)
Jerry Robinson *The Comics: An Illustrated History of Comic Strip Art* (Putnam, 1974)
Jeff Rovin *The Encyclopaedia of Superheroes* (Oxford, 1986)
Sue Sharpe *'Just Like a Girl': How Girls Learn to be Women* (Penguin, 1976)
Jeremy Tunstall *The Media in Britain* (Constable, 1983)
Cynthia L. White *Women's Magazines 1693-1968* (Michael Joseph, 1970)
Raymond Williams *The Long Revolution* (Pelican, 1961)

Picture acknowledgements
The author and publishers would like to thank the following for allowing their illustrations to be reproduced in this book: All-Sport 28; BBC Hulton Picture Library 4, 20, 35, 42-3; Mary Evans Picture Library 7-8, 14, 18, 31, 33; Health Education Authority 21 (below) photographed by Paul Seheult; John Frost Historical Newspaper Service 5, 10, 18, 21 (above) 27, 32 (10, 18, 21 (above), 27 photographed by Paul Seheult); The Mansell Collection 6 (above); Christine Osborne Pictures 12 (below); David Redfern 26; Paul Seheult cover, 9, 10, 13, 15 (below), 16, 19, 22 (above and below), 23, 25, 28, 30, 34, 37, 39, 40, 41, 44; John Topham Picture Library 6 (below); Wayland Picture Library 15 (above), 24, 29, 36; Tim Woodcock 11, 12 (above). The publishers would also like to thank Jump magazine for their help.

Index

Action Force 20
action comics 18
advertisements 6, 9, 13, 15, 29
alternative press 28-9, 40
Answers 8
Arena 37
Australia 23, 28; *Bluey and Curley* 19; *Cosmopolitan* 37; *Creem* 27; *Gentleman's Quarterly* 37; *Jane* 19; *New Musical Express* 27; *Ram* 27; *Reader's Digest* 9; *Smash Hits* 28; *2000* AD 23

Battle with Stormforce 23
Beano 20
Birchill, Julie 27
Black Beat 16
Blitz 29
boys' magazines 24-5
Brown, Tom 17
Bunty 24

Care Bears 20
cartoons 17, 18
Chic 16
Chicago America 18
Chick's Own 17
Children and Young People's Harmful Publications Act 46
circulation 7, 10, 39, 46
colour supplements 17, 40
Comic Cuts 8
comics 17-21, 41-2
computerized publishing 12-13
conglomerates 11, 46
consumers 9, 11, 46

D.C. Comics 41
Daily Mail 8
Daily Mirror 8
Dandy 20
Debbie 24
direct sales 41, 46
distribution 7, 14-15, 30

Eagle 20
Economist The 39
editors 11-12, 46
electronic magazine channels 10
Escape 42

The Face 29
facsimile 13, 46

Fairly Serious Monthly 25
Family Circle 34
fanzines 28, 46
fashions 29, 35
fax 13
features 46
Film Fun 17
free magazines 15, 30, 40
funnies 17

Gay News 40
Gentleman's Magazine 4
girls' magazines 24-5
Good Housekeeping 9, 33
glossies 28-29, 37, 46

Home Chat 8, 33
Honey 34
House of Dolls 28

ID 29
IPC 10-11
Illustrated Chips 17
Inky Fingers 11
International Thomson Organisation 11

Jackie 25
Jane 19
Judge Dredd 23
Just Seventeen 25

Kerrang! 30

Ladies Diary 31
Ladies Mercury 31
Ladies' Magazine 4
layout 12, 29, 46
leisure interest magazines 39-42
Living 34
Logan, Nick 29
London's Australasian Magazine 15
Love Affair 25
Love and Rockets 41

magazines 4, 6-9
Magnet 18
Mail on Sunday 40
Marvel comics 23, 41
Melody Maker 27
men's magazines 37
Mizz 25
Moore, Alan 42
Motorcycle News 24, 38
music magazines 26-7
My Lady's Novelette 33

National Magazine Company 11
National Readership Survey 13
A New England 28
new journalism 26
New Musical Express 27
New Statesman 39
Nova 36

Observer 40
opinion-forming journals 39
Options 37
Over 21 34

partworks 44, 46
Pearson's Weekly 8
penny dreadfuls 8, 46
Penthouse 42
photo-magazines 9, 22
Photolove 25
Picture Post 9
Plain Truth 15
Playboy 42
Practice 10
Prima 16
printing 6-7, 12-13
Private Eye 39
publishers 10-11, 46
Pulse 30

Radio Fun 17
Radio Times 38
Reader's Digest 9
readership research 11, 13, 29
Record 27
retailers 14-15, 30, 46
Retailing World 10
Romeo 34
Roy of the Rovers 22

Sanity 40
science fiction 23
service magazines 9, 33, 46
Seventeen 34
Shoot 22
Sky 29
Smash Hits 28
Spare Rib 35-6
special interest magazines 10, 24-5, 39-42
Spectator 39

sports magazines 38-9
stamp duty 6
Sub-Aqua Scene 38
subscriptions 14, 39
Sunday Times 40
Swamp Thing 42

tabloids 27, 46
teenage magazines 22-5
television 34, 39
Thomson, D.C. 20
tie-in 20, 46
Titbits 8
Time 9
Top 30
Tower record shops 30
trade magazines 11, 14
TV Comic 17
TV Times 38
2000 AD 23, 41
typesetting 12, 46

USA 7, 14, 17, 18, 19, 28; *Captain Easy* 19; *Cosmopolitan* 37; *Doonesbury* 20; *Ebony* 9; *Family Circle* 34; *The Fantastic Four* 20; *G.I. Joe* 20; *Gentleman's Quarterly* 37; *Good Housekeeping* 33; *House of Dolls* 28; *Jet* 9; *Ladies' Home Journal* 8; *Life* 9; *Little Orphan Annie* 18; *MS* 35; *McClures* 7; *Munsey's* 7; *Mutt and Jeff* 17, 18; *Negro Digest* 9; *New York World* 17; *Newsweek* 9, 39; *Peanuts* 20; *Pennsylvania Magazine* 6; *Reader's Digest* 9; *Romantic Confessions* 8; *Sports Illustrated* 39; *TV Guide* 38; *Teen* 34; *Time* 9, 39; *US News* 39; *Vogue* 33; *Woman's Home Companion* 33; *Woman's Journal* 33; *Working Woman* 37; *World Report* 39; *The Yellow Kid* 17

Valentine 34
video magazines 10
Vogue 33
The Voice 16

W.H. Smith 7
war comics 23
wholesalers 14-15
Wire 30
Woman 34
Women's Liberation 35
women's magazines 31-7
Working Woman 37